Write and Publish Books on Your Smartphone: Anywhere in the World

Calvin Jones

Published by Steve Jones, 2023.

WRITE AND PUBLISH BOOKS ON YOUR SMARTPHONE: ANYWHERE IN THE WORLD

First edition. October 4, 2023.

Copyright © 2023 Calvin Jones.

ISBN: 979-8223217916

Written by Calvin Jones.

Table of Contents

This short booklet is dedicated to all of you, who aspire to, and are working towards, becoming location, independe

This book documents - and represents the outcome of - my attempt to write, edit, format and publish a book purely using a smartphone. Because it tests the feasibility of editing on a phone, some typos will have slipped through. That's the point of the experiment!

Please do leave a review, including pointing out any errors. I really appreciate your feedback.

Please leave a review on your chosen bookstore website, as that helps others discover (or avoid!) this book.

Links to gear and software I used to write this book

Given that one of the main premises of this book is that I want to build multiple streams of income, it would be remiss of me not to include some affiliate links somewhere! So I provide links to some of the equipment and software mentioned in the book at my website at stevecjones.uk[1]

---

1. http://stevecjones.uk

1. Introduction

It's late April 2023. I'm sitting in a café in Ventnor on the Isle of Wight. It's raining outside. It's always raining! I'm cheesed off. I've been in the UK for just a bit too long and I need a change of scene. Although I've done a few extended trips abroad, and lived in Cambodia twice, collecting data on tiger prey of all things, so far I've followed the rather conventional route of getting a commute-to day job here in the UK, being tied to one town.

Now, though, I'm approaching middle-age. I'm wondering: *Do I really want to continue to follow the usual conventional lifestyle for life's second half?* Is there an alternative? Could I become a Digital Nomad? Location independent? And by doing that, could I live anywhere in the world, earning an income on the move, from the road?

At the beginning of 2023 I set myself a challenge: to create and run a business or two purely from my iPhone Mini 13. Side hustles that can be delivered while sat on a beach in Bali or trekking along a tropical forest trail in northern Thailand.

If that's possible, and I'm not sure it is, I might be able to live anywhere, embracing my nomadic tendencies, and still earn enough income to get by.

I've set up a couple of YouTube channel, the *Cornish Vandweller*, and *The iPhone Entrepreneur*, to document different aspects of my progress in video form. Those YouTube channels, and another channel focused on my obsession with travel and nature (*Steve Jones Wild Writer*), are part of my earning strategy.

I need to build *multiple* streams of income. Relying on just one when I really don't know the likely outcome is a recipe for failure. It leaves one vulnerable: if I'm in the middle of the Andes, relying on just one income stream, and that fails, I'm essentially screwed! Two or three sources of income is ideal, earning a third or quarter of what I need from each.

I've decided to try two business ideas initially. The first is to develop those YouTube channels. Can I set up, optimise, make decent video content for - and then monetise - three YouTube channels, just using my smartphone? By 'monetise' I mean via two means initially: Google AdSense and the Amazon Affiliate Programme.

The second smartphone venture, complimenting my YouTube channels, is book writing and independent book publishing.

Can I *write* a book manuscript on my phone, get it *edited*, get a decent *book cover*, *format* the book, get it *published*, and get it selling - just using my iPhone?

Are there limits to what one can really do with a compact smartphone in terms of video content creation and book writing and publishing? Just how far into those processes can I get?

This book is the output of the initial book writing experiment. A proof of concept, if you like.

Yes, I've written this book on my smartphone to document my investigation into whether it's possible to write a book on a phone...

But did I hit stumbling blocks? Did I resort to my MacBook Air to get it across the line?

Read on to find out how much of this book was actually created just using a smartphone, and how I went about the task...

2. A bit of context

The smartphone you doubtless already own is a miniaturised computer with the capability to do remarkable things.

My smartphone is an iPhone Mini 13, and I think it's the best phone ever created for the nomad. Like my phone, I'm something of a minimalist. I don't like to accumulate too much 'stuff'. I like to travel as light as possible. Traditionally, I've taken a laptop with me. Because I've been entrapped by Apple, my laptop-of-choice has been the MacBook Air. It's a lightweight device that has served me well while writing in small Colombian log cabins and forest camps in Cambodia.

But it's still more bulky than I'd like. And charging up a MacBook Air in a remote forest eight hours by dirt bike from the nearest wall socket has proven challenging at times.

In 2021, I shifted to an iPad Air with a Logitech Combo Touch case with keyboard. This combination served me well too. I've grown rather fond of the Logitech. Its large trackpad obviates the need for a mouse, and I appreciate the longer battery life of the iPad Air. I could use a small solar panel in a rainforest glade to top it up with juice, too. Trouble is, the rubber in the first generation of this Logitech isn't tough enough to withstand the tropical heat. It expands and contracts and got bent out of shape after just a couple of years of use. The second-generation Combo Touch is made of tougher stuff I gather.

Even that combination - iPad Air with Combo Touch - as nice as it is, is just a little bit too bulky!

In spring 2022, failing to live up to my clutter-free minimalist persona, I purchased an iPad Mini 6. Apart from the odd way in which the Apple iOS scrunches the app icons together on the home page, I love this little device. I found a nice little Arteck keyboard case for $19.99 online after viewing a review of it on the *Very Last Dollar* YouTube channel. This combination proved excellent, though not perfect. Because the 'tilt' of the keyboard case when open was slightly less than I wanted, making writing a little uncomfortable, I purchased a separate compact Gritin iPad stand online. Because the keyboard part of the case is detachable and connects via Bluetooth, the stand enables me to use the keyboard detached from the iPad Mini. This has worked nicely and, although the price of that keyboard case was inflated to a jaw-breaking $27.99 by May 2023, it remains a bargain and I have a spare on order.

But that little Arteck keyboard lacks a trackpad, so I found myself switching back to the iPad Air with Logitech keyboard for longer-form writing and easy screen navigation.

By now I'd amassed a warehouse size collection of gadgets and realised this wasn't serving my minimalist aspirations.

I'd yet to find my perfect, compact, multi-purpose work-while-traveling device.

A key change in mindset and approach is hinted at by the various *keyboard* cases mentioned above.

I was still *physically typing* my words... I had a blog: *typing*. I was a few hundred words into a book project: *typing*. How else is one to get their words down on paper, so to speak?

Then, in summer 2022, I finally discovered the voice-to-text functionality built into the Apple operating system. The kids tell me there's something similar built into Android devices. This stuff is second nature to most young people but I'm a middle-aged technophobe so voice-to-text was a revelation.

My voice-to-text writing adventure was chaotic at first. My early efforts revolved around drafting short pieces of five hundred words or less for my blog.

Initially, I spoke too fast and mumbled too much. The artificial intelligence running the voice-to-text function misinterpreted my words in hilarious ways and sometimes just gave up and buggered off. But, over the next couple of months, I started to perfect my approach. Things started to click. My AI buddy and I reached an accommodation and it started to comprehend what I was trying to say.

My un-typed upon keyboard cases started to gather dust.

This voice-to-text technique for short-form writing got me thinking: do I actually *need* to sit down at a desk with a keyboard and larger tablet or laptop to write *at all*? Can I ditch the keyboards, and the desk?

Could I use an even smaller device than the iPad Mini, with this voice-to-text functionality, to write not just short blog posts, but longer-form pieces? A book even? And from anywhere - during a walk in the park, while sat on the beach, while trekking through the Bornean rainforest, while on the loo even?!

Possibly, I thought. But what smaller device?

Well, in summer 2022 I purchased an iPhone Mini 13. I really purchased this for its video creation capabilities. My YouTube channels were beginning to gain some traction and

I wanted a device that was very compact and very good for shooting decent quality vlogs.

This beautiful, tiny phone also has the same voice-to-text capability built into the operating system as my iPads. And Scrivener, my go-to book-writing software, has an app for smartphones. So, in principle, I could write books on my phone in the same writing software I've been using on my MacBook Air and iPads.

So, I thought to myself, could this smartphone be the perfect mobile computer for writing the first draft of a book manuscript?

And just how far beyond writing a rough manuscript could this mini computer take me?

So was born my YouTube channel, *The iPhone Entrepreneur*.

On that channel I explore income streams one might generate using just a smartphone. I use my iPhone Mini 13 as the case study device.

This book reports one such experiment: to what extent is it possible to create a book on a phone?

If it's possible to write and publish one book, it's obviously possible to produce more books that way.

If those books start selling, one has a side-income. Just a trickle perhaps. But what if that side-income begins to ramp-up as more books are written and published? Clearly, by working from such a tiny device, one might be able to travel, writing and publishing books 'on the move', with sales helping to finance those travels.

Read on to discover how things have gone!

3. Book outline

This book aims to provide a 'chatty' account of what I've gone through to draft and edit a book manuscript (this book manuscript!), get it formatted initially as an ebook, then a paperback, and get it independently published. I'll run through each step I followed to get this book into your hands, from initially getting words from my head into my smartphone, to finally uploading a complete book file for publication on the Amazon platform.

Hopefully my informal account will go some way to revealing what's possible using just a smartphone, and will convince you to get your book written and published this way.

4. The manuscript drafting process

This section summarises the processes I went through to work out what to write about, and to create the draft manuscript of this book. I'll also cover some other key points, such as book length.

4.1 What are you writing about?

I needed to work out what to write! You'll need to do that too. Will you be writing fiction or non-fiction? I rarely read novels. I don't often read fiction of any sort.

This book is a work of non-fiction and I have a fair few book project ideas I want to tackle once this one is done.

I like science, particularly natural history. So I'll be writing natural science books after this one.

I'm also a vanlifer: that just means that I live in a van in the UK in the summer and hope to be able to live closer to the warmth of the tropics in our northern winter, between mid-November and the end of February.

So I have a few book ideas around these vanlife, location independence and travel niches.

Some people recommend 'writing to market'. That means working out what sorts of subjects are in high demand that a given time and writing books to meet those demands.

I suggest you write on subjects you're passionate about. This should ensure that you can keep going and get a few books under your belt. My own main niche, nature writing, isn't particularly large. So I'll only achieve relatively modest sales from each book I write. You might be lucky enough to be passionate about the subject with a file larger readership. If you hit that sweet spot, all power to you.

If you're planning on building a book writing and publishing *side income*, you'll need to write and publish several books. If you want to generate a *full-time living* from books, and that's certainly feasible, you'll need to publish quite a few books. My hope is that I'll generate around a third of my rather modest daily living costs from book sales.

Having a genuine interest in the subjects about which you're writing will help keep you motivated and improve your chance of success.

4.2 Book length

This book is very short. I prefer to *read* shorter books. But I also appreciate sitting down to read a good, long book while on holiday.

Because this book is essentially a 'how to' book, it needs to be succinct and to the point.

After this short book, my future projects will likely range anywhere between 15,000 words up to about 60,000. 30,000 words will probably be my sweet spot. But I will tend to focus on *shorter* books. You might consider going short for your first project too, so you can pass through the various steps from manuscript-drafting to publication relatively quickly. This should give you the confidence to know that book writing and publishing is straightforward.

4.3 Give your book project a name

I gave my book manuscript a working title (*'The iPhone Entrepreneur'*) and subtitle ('How to write and publish your books on a smartphone. From anywhere in the world!'). I did so without much thought. That'll do for now, surely?

I've just read a blog post explaining how important your book title is to discovery on online platforms. You need to try to work out what sorts of search terms people use when looking for the sorts of book you're writing. This will help the online algorithms to pitch your book more reliably to potential readers.

I'm also wondering if I might get some sort of copyright claim if I use iPhone in the title?

Being stubborn, I'm going to stick with that working book title for now. You, my readers, might find that I settled on a better title by the time this book is published, but, at the time of writing this section, I haven't.

Being in near-full control means I can change the book cover and content, **but not its title**, at any point after it's published. So I'll need to make sure I settle on a book title I like *before* I finally publish it.

I suggest you do some Googling and search YouTube for advice on optimising book titles.

4.4 Writing the manuscript

One needs to write a rough first draft. I'm obstinately committed to attempting to write this book using only the voice-to-text functionality on my iPhone.

First, though, we have a more pressing consideration: what software or app to use?

I'm sure one could write a book in Microsoft Word, or Google Docs. Some people certainly do. But there are more refined long-form writing software options that are popular with authors. And I've yet to try to write anything into MS Word on my phone.

I use Scrivener. That's probably the most popular software among full-time authors. There's a new writing tool called Atticus that's gaining in popularity as I write this in 2023. I might well end up switching to that piece of software because it has impressive book formatting functionality built-in, and book formatting is one of the more tricky tasks we'll encounter later in this book.

Scrivener has a slimmed down app version for smartphones. I'm currently sitting on the beach on the Isle of Wight using the voice-to-text function to write this section into Scrivener.

I'll upload some short Scrivener demonstration videos onto my YouTube channel at some point.

I strongly urge you to consider getting Scrivener. The version for an iPhone (and iPad) entails a one-off licence purchase costing $23.99 in the Apple App Store.

With Scrivener, you can save your writing projects into your phone's memory, or you can synchronise with Dropbox, so your projects are safely saved in the cloud. I write anywhere, then synchronise to the cloud in Dropbox when I come across wifi. You could use your mobile data to do this.

Right, I've had Scrivener installed onto my iPhone for a few weeks. Let's get real about the state of the sentences generated via voice-to-text. I estimate it's about 95% accurate.

Unlike me, voice-to-text dictation doesn't make spelling mistakes. As long as it understands the words being spoken, it gets the spelling right. This is a massive bonus for me, because my spellings are usually wrong!

You *must* enunciate words clearly. If your phone doesn't hear you properly, the voice-to-text function can get the word wrong. I walk around my local beach and along the sea cliffs talking at my phone. I look like a bit of a moron but it's effective and better than being sat in a cafe or office. However, if it's blustery, voice-to-text is barely worth bothering with. So I write in sheltered spots or on still days. Or I use an external Bluetooth microphone. I use the fairly expensive dji mini microphone. This entails a receiver being plugged into the phone, with the microphone unit either being held or clipped onto my shirt close to my mouth. It works a treat. Much cheaper lavaliere microphones do just as good a job when used for dictation.

Some similar-sounding words can stump voice-to-text however clearly they're spoken. The software appears to understand sentences, so will get, say, *there* and *their* right. But, as far as I can see, it can't distinguish, say, *steal* and *steel*. Hopefully the artificial intelligence (AI) driving voice-to-text will get even better through time.

At the editing stage I'll have to be really careful to pick up these sorts of errors.

You can tell me how well I've done in the reviews....

A really striking benefit of voice-to-text over conventional typing is the sheer speed. People can generally speak far more quickly than they can type.

The trick is to talk very, very clearly. You don't need to talk *slowly*. Just very *clearly*. Again, annunciate words correctly. I found it took me a few weeks to get my speaking pace just right but once I'd nailed it I found this approach to work a treat. It's also worth bearing in mind that this sort of dictation can be surprisingly tiring initially. Normal speaking isn't gruelling: getting thoughts down using voice-to-text can be until you're used to it. I gather audiobook narration is equally tiring.

Mostly, I open the Scivener app, open my writing project in it, activate the on-screen keyboard, and then press the microphone button in the bottom right corner of the on-screen keyboard. I then proceed to speak and my words are rendered into the manuscript.

I've also found that I can whisper barely audibly into the dji Bluetooth microphone when in cafes and it'll still render my voice as text very well. No need to speak loudly when using an external mic. So I've started to find quiet corners in pubs and cafes on rainy days where I sit and quietly write, without the need for a laptop.

Now that I'm in my writing flow state, I can easily write a thousand words in an hour using voice-to-text, usually while walking along the coastal path or while sat down in a cove. I do ten minute writing sprints with a five minute break between each.

I've only been writing for about two hours daily. In principle, a ten-thousand word manuscript can be drafted in less than ten days, across rather fewer than ten hours, if writing one or two thousand words daily.

But I've been doing quite a bit of research during the writing process. Writing and research amounts to about three hours daily.

A fair bit of background research for this book was done by listening to various podcasts, and reading blogs. That's all straightforward on a smartphone. I usually use the reading pane on my web browser to render blog posts more readable on my phone screen. I can also send such posts to my Kindle app on my phone. That means I can adjust text size further and it makes reading very easy.

Clearly, working just two or three hours daily on book-writing is the barest minimum. I'll undoubtedly ramp-up my writing as the summer progresses, probably writing for four or five hours daily. In principle I should be able to get eight to ten thousand words written most days.

To round this section off, yes, I did manage to get a rough draft of this book manuscript finished on my iPhone.

But it needed some editing...

4.5 Editing the manuscript

Okay, so it's mid May and I have the first rough draft of this book written. I still can't believe I've managed to draft it all on my phone. I've read through the initial draft and I'm impressed how straightforward it's been to get it this far.

But it really is just a *rough* draft. It needs quite a bit of work still. I'm reasonably happy with the overall flow and the general content. But it needs editing.

Book-editing is a highly skilled process demanding talents I lack.

My spelling is awful and my grasp of English grammar is tenuous at best. Thankfully, voice-to-text helps to address my dodgy spelling. But grammar? Who knows?!

That's the problem: if you've never really learnt (or is that learned?!) grammar it can be very difficult to pick out your own errors. My manuscript will thus need a proper edit.

How?

Does it count if I send my draft, written on my phone, away to an editor who'll most likely use a laptop to work on it? There are loads of freelancers so finding one isn't a problem. The *Alliance of Independent Authors* has a whole directory full of the names of digital nomads making a living as freelance book editors. Maybe I can spend a bit and commission one of those editors?

The whole point of my YouTube channel, and the account in this book, is to see whether I can write *and* edit *and* publish books *purely on my phone.* That includes every step in the process.

So, to honour the spirit of the experiment, I should first try to edit it myself on my phone.

I've got about a third of the way through the manuscript. I've found that I can read the manuscript and correct errors or add in or remove bits of text using both the voice-to-text and keyboard functionality in the phone. Screen size is fine, for me at least. You can increase text size within Scrivener, so reading isn't a problem as long as the sun isn't too bright.

I'm quite sure that I'm missing errors. But I'm enjoying the editing process. I've done short editing sprints while waiting in line to buy a gig ticket, while on the loo, on the bus and on the beach.

Fast-forward a week. I now have what I think is a relatively clean manuscript.

I've discovered an additional editing technique. I can send a copy of the manuscript in *docx* format across to the Kindle app on my phone. There, I can view the draft as if it's a finished ebook. I read through, and each time I spot an error, or a piece of text I want to adjust, I simply highlight it. Then, I return to the manuscript within Scrivener and address the highlights in my Kindle version.

This additional editing step is great, because it enables me to read my manuscript as others will read the final product, as an ebook.

To get the draft manuscript from the Scrivener app on my phone onto the Kindle app on the phone, I use the compile function within Scrivener. This function allows one to compile the manuscript into a Word style document (i.e. the *docx* file.) One can then press the little 'send' button within Scrivener, and send it straight to your Kindle app. Obviously to do this you need to have the Kindle app downloaded onto your phone. It's free.

Okay, we're almost there.

What I probably ought do now, with my manuscript as 'clean' as I'm able to get it, is to email it over to a freelance line editor. But I won't.

A good thing about short non-fiction writing, like this book, is that the structure is relatively straightforward. I'm not writing a novel. Or a long narrative non-fiction book with a complex storyline. So the editing process feels relatively straightforward.

In the end, I *did* edit this book myself entirely on my phone.

I'm inclined to think that emailing future manuscripts to a freelance editor would respect the spirit of *The iPhone Entrepreneur*. But I very much doubt the editor would also be using a smartphone.

Anyway, we have proof of concept. I'll leave you to spot the remaining errors and point them out to me in the reviews.

Deep breath.

At this point, if I was relying on a traditional publisher, I'd send my draft manuscript off to them and wait. I'd probably wait for a good year, most likely more, before the book finally appears for sale.

But I'm fully independent. I'm going to publish this book myself. I can do that far, far more rapidly than any traditional publishing house.

So... now I need to format my finished manuscript to turn it into an actual book...

23

Write your notes below: did you manage to write and edit your book on your phone? Jot down any stumbling blocks so you remember how you addressed them for the next book...

24

5. From manuscript to formatted book

I'm impressed by how far I've managed to get in the process so far. Question is, can I convert my finished manuscript into a book file that can actually be published?

5.1 What book format?

There are three main classes of format that I'll be considering for my own books: ebook, printed book (paperback and hardcover), and audiobook.

Initially, I'd intended to try all formats straight away. But I've decided just to go with ebook and paperback versions for now. Maybe I'll try to create a hardback book and record an audiobook version later. Alternatively, I'll turn my attention to writing my next book.

Let's look at creating an ebook first, then we'll consider printed formats in Section 9.

5.2 Creating an ebook file

Let's look first at creating an ebook. By 'ebook' I mean an EPUB file viewable on e-readers like Kindles, Nooks etc, and associated apps that enable you to read those books on a PC, laptop or tablet computer. I'll not address PDF formatting because, although it's a very easy format to create and work with, actually getting it to a purchaser is, I gather, a little more complicated.

I'll look at getting the ebook out first because ebooks are I think the biggest selling book format, and they also appear to be a straightforward format to work with and get published quickly.

As ever, I do have the option of emailing my finished manuscript and book cover to a book formatting freelancer. Again, the Alliance of Independent Authors has a whole directory full of the contact details of such freelancers. But let's first explore options for doing this myself on my phone.

Ideally, I'd like to do it quickly and for free. Is there software for this? Vellum is widely recommended for converting a manuscript into an ebook file, but it's not an option because there's no iPhone app (it's very good though and is available for the Mac). Atticus is a new piece of writing software that has an excellent formatting function built in. But, again, I don't think I can use that effectively on a tiny smartphone screen.

Draft2Digital has book formatting functionality that looks like a good bet too. It's a popular platform with independent book authors and is run by writers. Let's give that a go.

My manuscript is loitering in Scrivener. It's simple in that it has one consistent text style for chapter headings, another style for sub-headings, and another for the main body text. I need to make sure the format of all three text elements is consistent throughout as that'll make life easier when it comes to converting it into an EPUB file.

First, I need to extract my finished manuscript from Scrivener. I use the Compile function within Scrivener and save the manuscript as a *docx* file within the Files app on my phone.

That took seconds and was easy.

Now, let's look at the Draft2Digital platform. Just type that into your browser or Google to find their website.

To get going I needed to set up a free Draft2 Digital account. That takes a minute or two. All one needs initially is an email address and password. Registering and the subsequent process I'll be going through below is entirely free. You'll need to do that to perform the following steps.

I'm taken to my account page where there's a big red button at the top that reads:

MY BOOKS

Hit the tab and you'll be presented with another red button, *'ADD NEW BOOK'*. Once you have been through this process with a few books in Draft2Digital, you'll also have a list of your existing book projects below that 'add book' button. At the moment, just hit 'Add new book' and that'll take you to a page where you can either 'start ebook' or 'start print book'.

Now, you're invited to either upload your book cover or wait if you don't yet have it.

I fill in a few boxes: book name; publisher name; author name (one can use a pseudonym; I have!); search terms (the sorts of terms people might use for online searches when trying to find a book in a particular genre or in a particular subject area. So, say 'write a book on an iPhone', and 'self-publish a book'); etc.

It's all pretty self-explanatory and I can return later to tweak and embellish this information.

After filling in a few more boxes of information, I'm asked to upload the manuscript file. I navigate to the *docx* formatted document in the Files app on the phone and it uploads in under a minute.

You're then able to preview the uploaded book file.

I'm impressed: Draft2Digital has recognised the chapter headings and sub-headings I generated within Scrivener.

We just have a few more straightforward boxes to fill in. If you're trying this at home and are getting stuck, do a YouTube tutorial search. There are a few that walk you through the process. This website is constantly improving its interface so things will have changed by the time you read this: just use their Help menu if you get stuck, or search YouTube.

The Draft2Digital preview tool allows you to examine your ebook using its default template. You can switch through several template styles. You see on the screen a rendering of your book as if you're looking at an e-reader. It's pretty cool, if a little difficult to view on a smartphone screen...

Try each template and settle on one. You can then customise further to a limited extent within your chosen template. Again, this is covered in various YouTube tutorials.

Eventually, after well under half an hour, I've filled in all the required information and I have an ebook file saved within my Draft2Digital account, formatted just as I want it.

I can now download a copy of this finished file onto my phone Files app. That's all completely free. In the next step I'll be creating an ebook cover and I'll save that as a separate file in the same place.

Later, I'll return to Draft2Digital because it's primarily a book distributor through which I can get my book published on lots of platforms. So I can get my ebook onto the website of many retailers, not just one.

Having downloaded my formatted ebook file, I sent a copy over to my Kindle app to have a browse of the finished book on my phone.

It worked!

5.3 Designing an ebook cover

Now, I need a cover for my ebook ready for when I upload my book for publication.

One of the first rules of independently publishing books is: ***don't design your own book cover***, unless you're a skilful book cover designer!

Like editing, book cover design is a whole, skilled profession in its own right.

And getting a really good book cover design is absolutely crucial to getting sales. Like it or not, people *really do* judge a book by its cover. It's not so much that they decide whether or not to buy it based on the cover. It's really a question of whether they decide to *look inside at all*.

The cover acts a bit like a tap on the shoulder. If you manage to catch someone's eye as they scan a shelf of books, they might pick your book up and have a look at the blurb on the back and a few pages inside.

They literally do that in a real bookshop. They do something similar online: they'll click on your thumbnail-size book cover image, read the blurb on the sales page and, if you're lucky, they'll order a copy.

Or they might download a free sample (highlighting the importance of the first few pages of text: make sure you get some decent written material within that viewable sample at the beginning of your book).

Go onto Amazon, search for a book, and click 'look inside' to see what's viewable in the sample. If all you can view within this sample is a copyright page and the contents, you don't really get a good idea about the quality of the writing. So I'll be making sure the text of this book starts within the first two or three pages so people can read some of it in the sample.

Anyway, to re-iterate the correct advice: don't attempt to design your own book cover, and absolutely don't attempt it on your smartphone.

Let's ignore that advice for now!

I'm going to use the free software application called Canva. Google it. It's excellent and versatile.

You need to register an account to start using Canva. I registered for the free version. A paid subscription is excellent value for money, but I'll reserve that for when I start earning money from book sales.

A quick search of Canva reveals a whole load of book cover design templates that you can use as a starting point. Some are free to use, some require a paid subscription. For now, I'll use one of the free templates. I kept the template and text style, added some free images and changed the text.

You can tell me whether this rather slap dash, 'do it yourself' approach was a good idea!

There's another free option. Amazon's Kindle Direct Publishing (KDP) platform has a book cover design function. When you come to upload your completed manuscript to the Amazon KDP platform (we'll get to that soon!), you'll be asked to either upload your own cover or use Amazon's built-in cover design tool to create one.

I chose to play around with Canva, but Amazon's tool is straightforward and can yield very basic covers from a very limited set of rather poor templates.

Because I have complete control as an independent writer and publisher, I can easily change the book cover after the book is published. If it sells, I might even have enough money to invest in getting a freelancer to design a new cover for me!

That's essentially the plan: write and independently publish a few books, and then, if they start to generate an income, reinvest some of that money back into the book business.

For now, though, I've designed my own ebook cover in Canva on my smartphone. There's a search bar at the top of the Canva account page once you're logged in. There, I typed 'ebook cover' at was presented with a range of ebook cover templates. I picked one of the free options, deleted its cover art and added some free images from the Canva library, and re-worded the book title, author name etc. After I was done, I clicked to download as a print PDF document. I downloaded it from Canva and saved it into my Files app on the phone, alongside but separate from the ebook file.

6. A quick stock take

Just one month into my *iPhone Entrepreneur* experiment I now have a finished book manuscript, with a book cover I designed myself, and an ebook file ready for publication.

And it's a book I've written, edited and formatted entirely using my phone.

But creating a digital product like this means nothing if I can't get it published.

In the following sections I'll outline how I went about getting the ebook published. Thankfully, this proved to be straightforward.

7. Getting the ebook published

Now I need to decide where, amongst the whole variety of options, I want to publish my ebook.

7.1 Where to publish?

In his self-published book *Write Your Book on the Side*, Hassan Osman suggests that, as a first time, independent author, you might consider publishing your ebook exclusively through Kindle Select on the Amazon Kindle Direct Publishing (KDP) platform.

By signing up to Kindle Select you agree initially to sell the ebook version only on Amazon to users of Kindle devices and the Kindle app on their phones and tablets computers. That latter bit is important: anyone can read Kindle books if they download the Kindle app onto their phone or tablet. That's a very large potential readership.

You get a few perks for signing onto Kindle Select, and you can leave the agreement after 90 days and publish more widely, or extend for a further 90 days, and so on.

You're still free to publish paperback, hardback and audiobook versions on Amazon and other platforms because KDP Kindle Select only applies to the ebook version.

Alternatively, you can 'go wide' with the ebook from the start: in other words, publish on all online retail stores, not just Amazon, and also on your own website. Most independent writers recommend going wide eventually. But it's fine to start off exclusively with Kindle Select. So that's what I'm going to do.

7.2 Publishing the ebook on Amazon

Amazon is the world's biggest bookstore. Whether we like it or not, most books are purchased on Amazon, and that's where you as an author will probably see most sales. And getting my book onto Amazon's marketplace is the most straightforward first step.

The question, of course, is: can I do all that I need to do to get it published on Amazon just using my smartphone?

I soon discover that this process is very quick, very straightforward and free.

It's only at the point of sale that Amazon takes its relatively modest cut (relative to the amount a traditional publisher would take).

Let's just hover there for a moment. What do I mean by a *relatively modest* cut? Essentially, Amazon is acting as a storefront on your behalf. Whereas a traditional publisher will take around 85% to 90% of the cover price for each book sold, Amazon takes 30% if you publish yourself on its platform, and if you price your book at between $2.99 and $9.99.

So, you get 70% if you do it yourself, but just c.10% if you work with a traditional publisher.

I'll go ahead and publish on Amazon's Kindle Select. Here's the process I went through.

First, I logged in to Amazon KDP using my existing Amazon shopping account. If you don't buy things from Amazon, and don't have an account set up, you'll need to do that now. It's easy to do. If you're not keen on Amazon out of principle I suggest you get over it. Just do a Google search for Amazon KDP to find the login page.

Amazon KDP will walk you through a number of steps. The information requested should be fairly straightforward to provide. And if you get stuck, and I doubt you will, there are plenty of online forums and YouTube videos explaining the process. But it really is pretty self-explanatory.

You'll be invited to upload your completed manuscript and book cover. Perhaps oddly, I decided *not* to use the EPUB file I created via Draft2Digital earlier, because I wanted to see if I could do everything via the Amazon KDP platform. So I uploaded the *docx* file instead. That worked very well: the ebook creation tool within KDP works just as well as that provided by Draft2Digital.

I then uploaded the print PDF ebook cover I'd created in Canva. That, too, worked just fine.

I was required to press the 'previewer' button. This is a tool Amazon includes that allows you to view your completed ebook file rendered onto a mock e-reader before you finally publish. I opened the previewer and it all looked good.

One section that is more complicated to complete and requires some forethought is the book description. This is the blurb that potential buyers will encounter when they look at your book details on the Amazon store front.

I spent some time preparing this text before I logged into Amazon KDP. There's a small cottage industry of YouTube channels and paid services out there to help you with this aspect. Getting this blurb, or sales pitch, right can really boost the number of books you sell. So it's worth spending a bit of time on it.

I came up with my own blurb. That will probably do in the first instance, but I may go back and do some more research on this aspect later, once the book is up for sale. If my book sales really take off, once I have a few published, I'll probably go back and commission a freelancer to help me produce blurbs for each of my books.

Or I'll use ChatGPT... that's a whole topic I'll return to in a future book!

A key point here is that you are in control of (nearly) everything. You can go back into your account and change whatever you need to - apart from the book title and some other key bits of data that are carved in stone once you press the publish button - at a later date. You can upload a revised manuscript or book cover, or both, including updated additions, after you've published if you need to.

If, for example, reviewers point out grammatical errors, you can go back, correct the errors in your manuscript, and upload the corrected version. I strongly urge you to get your manuscript as good as possible *before you publish* though, because an error-strewn ebook is just asking for bad reviews, and it'll rightly get them!

Before you can press the publish button, Amazon will ask you to set the ebook price. I'll cover that in the next section.

7.3 Ebook pricing

How did I decide on my pricing?

If I price my book between $2.99 and $9.99, Amazon receives a 30% cut of the cover price, I get 70%. If I price below or above that range, Amazon gives me a 35% cut of the cover price and pockets the rest itself.

I've priced this ebook at $2.99. Experienced independent authors suggest that $2.99 is one of the sweet spots for pricing.

Some independent authors have found success pricing their ebooks somewhat higher.

The best strategy appears to be to experiment. $2.99 is the lowest I can price my book at and still receive 70% of the cover price. I'm going to start at $2.99, and perhaps increase or reduce the price later depending on how things go in the first few weeks.

7.4 Pressing publish...

I've arrived at the end of the boxes that need filling in on Amazon's publishing platform. Now I'm confronted by a prominent and ominous button:

PUBLISH...

I press it.

A dialogue box appears telling me the process has been successful and my book will be checked and will appear for sale on Amazon within between four and thirty-six hours assuming no problems are encountered!

I can't really believe it. I've written, edited, designed the cover for and now published an ebook on Amazon. Using just a smartphone.

7.5 Publishing more widely

Having watched various self-publishing videos on YouTube, it seems fairly clear that most authors prefer to publish on more than just Amazon.

I've chosen to publish *the ebook* exclusively on Kindle Select initially, but I can opt out of this after 90 days and then publish the ebook more widely.

And remember, Kindle Select exclusivity *only applies to the ebook version*.

So you have a choice. You could publish your ebook exclusively on Amazon for an initial 90 day period, and publish a paperback version on Amazon and all other online retail stores at the same time. Or you can publish all formats of your book widely, opting out of KDP Select.

I've decided just to enrol my ebook into Kindle Select for now. I'll publish a paperback version next. We'll move onto that shortly.

Your notes: was the ebook publishing process easier than you thought?

8. Another stock take

Given that my approach to publishing means I can avoid having any stock, any inventory, it might seem odd to have another stock take!

Anyway, where are we?

We've managed to get the finished manuscript and its cover formatted into an e-book. That ebook has been enrolled into Amazon's Kindle Select programme.

I go for a beer.

The next morning, I find an email from Amazon saying that my ebook has been successfully published! The ebook is now up for sale on Amazon and available within Amazon's Kindle Unlimited store.

And you're reading it...

I'll call that a win!

Everything has been done on my smartphone.

Now, we have the option of publishing a printed version of the book.

9. Paperback and hardback?

That's the ebook done. What about other formats? Surely creating printed versions of my book will be far more complicated, and will certainly demand a 'proper' computer?

Paperback

To publish a paperback version of my book I'll need to generate both a formatted interior and a new book cover. I'll cover those two steps below in turn.

Formatting the interior manuscript. At this stage in the process I'd started to investigate some versatile book manuscript formatting software including Vellum and Atticus. But, as far as I could see, neither can really be used effectively on a smartphone.

So I opted to create a paperback interior book file on Draft2Digital.

I went back into my account. I then navigated to my tap for this book. This tab already existed because I'd already uploaded and formatted the ebook version.

Here, I've given the option to create a paperback version of the book. I clicked that button. And then asked to upload the interior book file. I navigate back to my *docx* file, the same one I used to create the ebook. I uploaded this as prompted. Most of the information was already filled in, haven't been pulled across from the ebook version.

I was invited to preview the various templates available for a paperback book. Here, I experimented. I explored the various options provided by draft to digital, and the, admittedly fairly limited, options for adapting each of the templates. After some experimentation, I settled on the template you can now see if you're reading the paperback version of this book. I undertook a few of those limited available tweaks.

Your thing given the option of downloading a copy of your formatted paperback manuscript. I did this, and opened it in a PDF reader on my phone.

Checking through the initial downloading manuscript, I spotted a couple of errors, and identified some straightforward improvements. This entailed tweaking the *docx* file, which was straightforward. And then re-uploaded this and applied the template.

After a few attempts, I finally arrived at a PDF file that I was happy with.

Creating a book cover. Again, I decided to defy the unwritten rule of not designing your own book cover.

Amazon is very precise about the dimensions of a cover given the number of pages and the dimensions you want your book to be printed in. Within your KDP account, you'll find an area where you can specify those attributes and download a special template PDF. This is easy to find. Once you've entered the details requested and downloaded your PDF template, you can go to Canva and use that template to design your paperback book cover.

Haven't done this, I went back to Canva. I uploaded the template, and this generated a canvas upon which I could lay the elements of both the front cover and the back cover. My particular book doesn't have a spine because it's very short.

The front cover of the paperback version, I simply uploaded the image I used for the ebook. This was positioned appropriately, in the right hand section of the cover template.

I don't added some text to the back cover of the book, on the left-hand side of the template. For the back cover it's very important to remember that Amazon will add a barcode. The air of this barcode is clearly indicated on the template. Leave this area blank.

After awhile, experimenting with various different fonts and text colour, I was satisfied with what I had.

I downloaded a copy of the finished book cover by pressing the appropriate tab within Canva and selecting to download it as a print PDF document. That's the same format I used for the e-book cover. It's a format required by Amazon.

I saved my finalised paperback book cover in the Files app alongside my interior PDF file.

Now we're ready to attempt to publish the paperback on Amazon.

Publishing on Amazon. I went back into my Amazon KDP account, where I navigated to the option to create a paperback version of the ebook I'd already published. Amazon makes this extremely clear and obvious: they obviously want you to publish a paperback as well as an ebook!

Most of the important information for the paperback version was already carried through from the information I entered for the ebook.

I was invited to upload the interior PDF file. This took about a minute. Next, I was asked whether I had my own book cover ready to upload, or whether I'd like to use Amazon's book cover design feature. I opted to upload my own cover, navigating to the print PDF file I'd previously created in Canva.

With those files uploaded successfully, Amazon once again requires you to open your files in its previewer.

I did this, flicking through the resulting book, with cover attached, everything looks good to me. I approved the result, and Amazon proceeded to save the digital version of my paperback.

Once this step was complete, Amazon advised of the printing cost per book. For this particular book, that comes out at about $1.90. This sum is retained by Amazon to cover the print on demand operation they use to deliver my books to purchasers.

Within keen to pricing. I opted to price this particular book at $4.99. The printing cost is subtracted from that sum initially, and then receive 60% of what's left.

Having confirmed my pricing, I was invited to press publish. I did this, and a dialogue box appeared stating that the process had been successful, and, pending some checks by the Amazon team, my book would appear for sale from anywhere between four and thirty six hours.

Concluding thoughts. Hopefully you can see that the process of creating and publishing a paperback within Amazon is just a straightforward as that for creating an e-book. There's absolutely no reason not to create a paperback version as well as an ebook version.

Because Amazon uses print on demand, there's no inventory for me to worry about. Amazon takes care of all the fulfilment in return for the cut they take as each book is sold. I think that's a very good way of doing things because the thought of having to store a print run of books at home (in my van in other words) and then post them off to people as they're ordered terrifies me!

Hardback

My first genuine stumbling block! Amazon and many online retailers and other booksellers require a certain minimum page count to allow publication as a hardcover book. This particular book falls just short of that minimum page count. I'll therefore not progress a hardcover version at this stage. I will be looking at it for future books though. What I can say, though, is that the process on Amazon is just a straightforward as it proved to be for the paperback version. There are differences: the Amazon template for the hardback book cover is tailor-made, so you can't simply use the paperback templates. You effectively need to construct a fresh cover just for the hardback version. Apart from that, the process is pretty much the same, and as quick, as for the paperback format.

How about an audiobook?

I haven't yet attempted to get an audio version of this book created. I will quite soon. I'll attempt to record it myself, using my own voice, rather than commissioning a professional narrator. But there is added complexity. I see no reason why, with a decent microphone, I won't be able to record audio directly into this iPhone. But subsequent work on the audio file may be beyond its capability. I don't yet know. Oh, and AI-based narration seems to be getting really quite good. So I might explore options for getting an AI narrator to create the audiobook.

10 Will my books sell?

I successfully met my own challenge: I've written, edited, formatted, created a book cover for, and published both an ebook and a paperback book just on a smart phone.

But this isn't an ego trip, or a passion project. The real question is this: *is it possible to be an iPhone Entrepreneur?*

In other words, *can I actually set up and run a business on my smartphone?*

In those terms at least, writing a book is pointless if it doesn't contribute a stream of income that more than offsets the costs in terms of gear and my time invested in writing it.

I'm hoping that my book title, and the keywords and categories I selected when publishing my book on Amazon KDP Select, will send the algorithm adverts to the intended readership. But relying on that alone to publicise my book is unlikely to be particularly successful.

Promoting one's own independently-published books is a whole new skill set I need to learn. For now, I'm happy simply to have got my book onto the Amazon platform. I now want to drink my beer before it gets warm.

11 Onto the next book

I hope this first book written on my phone has convince you that creating a book writing business on your smartphone is possible.

This being the case, I think the potential is endless.

This book is rather short. But the process I've used to create the manuscript can readily be used to write longer books.

And why stop at one book? This book alone will probably only generate a tiny trickle of income. The trick is to have multiple books written and published. Each of those will provide its own trickle of income. Combined, you might start to see some respectable money coming in. And maybe a full-time income. It's for obviously take me a bit of time to build up a catalogue of books. But once they're written and published, they will continue to yield an income in the longer term, with little effort required by me, especially once the book marketing algorithms on Amazon start to learn who my leadership is.

So my plan now is to write a series of books on my phone.

What about you?

Clearly, to have the motivation and stamina to write multiple books, you need to enjoy writing. I love writing. And yes, I do have lots of ideas for additional books!

12 Conclusion

Although writing this manuscript proved to be one of the most straightforward bits of the process, all stages proved pretty tractable.

Getting the manuscript edited, converting it into an e-book file, and designing the book cover myself were probably the more tricky elements of the process.

But even those components really were pretty straightforward. As my writing business develops, hopefully I'll have funds available to commission editors and book cover designers. That's not cheating. I can email the manuscript from the iPhone to the editor!

And similarly I can commission a book cover designer entirely using my iPhone. So I think doing so remains within the spirit of this challenge.

I'd strongly urge any aspiring smartphone book writer to attempt to master voice-to-text transcription as a means of writing a draft manuscript. This technique has been a revelation. It can be tiring at first. And it takes a little time to master the art of correct pacing and clear annunciation. But it's worth the effort.

The the name of my *iPhone Entrepreneur* YouTube channel, and the challenge I've set myself for 2023, goes beyond just writing a book. I'm aiming to test and demonstrate whether or not it is possible to earn a full-time living from an iPhone.

This is why we needed to define what I mean by a full-time living.

I'm a minimalist. My expenses are very low. So the amount I need to earn to live a good life may well be somewhat lower than you.

Before you can address the question: *Can you earn a full-time income from your phone?*, you need to work out how much you actually need to live on.

All I can do in this book is report the practical feasibility of writing books on an smartphone.

As I write this, at the end of May 2023, I've set about writing my second book. That book will take a look at the various streams of income I'll be attempting to develop during 2023.

Fingers crossed, by the end of 2023, I'll be earning enough to start to live a location independent lifestyle.

Good luck with your own ventures!

13 Acknowledgements

First, thanks to the owners and staff at Besty & Spinky, the cafe in Ventnor Bay, Isle of Wight, England, that's kept me supplied with strong filter coffee every morning over the years.

Blakes tea hut on Ventnor beach keeps me hydrated with the best oat lattes in town (try their Puro coffee), and late afternoon oat milk teas at Toni's Tea Room is a ritual I hate to miss.

Thanks to my various friends in Ventnor for the banter.

Thanks to my late father: your obsession with gadgets clearly rubbed off on me! And to my always-patient mother for absorbing my grumpiness. To my sister, and Richard, and Adam, for always covering the pub bill....this time next year....

And to Kirsty, for being a lovely friend.

To Amy, a much-missed friend.

My other books

At the time of writing (September 2023), I've written and published six books, two under my pen name, Calvin Jones, and four under my real name, Steve Jones. All can be found on online bookstores and are listed below:

By Calvin Jones

Breaking Free in 2023

Write and Publish Books on Your Smartphone

By Steve Jones

Wildlife Watching Around Ventnor, Isle of Wight

Bird Watching Around Ventnor, Isle of Wight

Writers in the Wild

Creating Shrike Shrublands

I plan to write and publish several more books during 2023, and many more thereafter.

If you enjoyed reading this book do please consider leaving an honest review on Amazon. It helps their algorithm find potential readers.

Further notes: *summarise your experience so far*

Also by Calvin Jones

Write and Publish Books on Your Smartphone: Anywhere in the World

Watch for more at Stevecjones.uk.

About the Author

Calvin Jones is a nature and travel writer, living in his tiny Citroen Berlingo van in the UK during the summer months, and as close as possible to the tropics as soon as the first frosts hit the grass in England.

Read more at Stevecjones.uk.